KERRISDALE ELEGIES

George Bowering

TALONBOOKS

Talonbooks
P.O. Box 2076, Vancouver, British Columbia, Canada V6B 3S3
www.talonbooks.com

Typeset in Adobe Garamond and printed and bound in Canada.

First Printing: 2008

The publisher gratefully acknowledges the financial support of the Canada Council for the
Arts; the Government of Canada through the Book Publishing Industry Development Program;
and the Province of British Columbia through the British Columbia Arts Council and the Book
Publishing Tax Credit for our publishing activities.

LIBRARY AND ARCHIVES CANADA CATALOGUING IN PUBLICATION

Bowering, George, 1935–
        Kerrisdale elegies / George Bowering. — 2nd ed.

Poems.
ISBN 978-0-88922-590-9

        I. Title.

PS8503.O875K4 2008   C811'.54   C2008-903036-2

Here a star, and there a star,
  Some Lose their way.
Here a mist, and there a mist:
  Afterwards – day!

EMILY DICKINSON

Elegy One

If I did complain, who among my friends
would hear?
            If one of them
amazed me with an embrace
he would find his arms empty, his own face
staring from a mirror.

Beauty is the first prod of fear,
                                we must
live our lives in.
                We reach for her,
we think we love her, because she holds the knife
a knife-edge from our throat.
                                Every fair heart
is frightful.
                Every rose petal
exudes poison in bright sunlight.

So I close my mouth, and my cry
makes dark music in my belly.
                              Who would listen
who could amaze?
                        Friends and beauty
lie waiting in poems, and the god
whose life we once wrote has left us
to muck in a world we covered with grease.

        Maybe I should watch the blossoms
turn to toasted flakes on my cherry tree.
Maybe I should walk along 41st Avenue
where mothers in velvet jogging suits push prams
and imitate the objects of my first lyrics.
Maybe I should comb my hair
the way I did in high school.

In the night the wind slides in from the sea
and eats at our faces;
                        that sweetheart,
she would do anything you ask her,
ask her,
            she'll lie down for a lonely heart.
Night-time's for lovers, maybe, closing their eyes
and pretending tomorrow will be splendid.

You should know that, you adult;
why dont you fling your arms wide
into the juicy air, chuck your ardent loneliness,
bump birds out of their dark paths
homeward to their grieving chicks.

Be grateful –
                    sadness makes music, cruel
April tuned a string for you.
                              Moons
whirled around planets waiting for you to spot them.
The middle of the Pacific prepared a wave
to plash ashore at your visit.
                              A radio
switched to melody as you walked by
a neighbour's window.

You should know by now,
                    the world waited
to come alive at your step –
                              could you handle that?
Or did you think this was love,
                              movie music
introducing a maiden you could rescue?
Where were you going to keep her,
                              and keep her
from seeing those dreams you were already
playing house with?

When your heart hungers,
                    sing a song of six-
teen, remember your own maidenly love
and the girls that aroused it,
                          make them famous.
Remember their plain friends who danced so well
because they never got into a back seat.
Bring them all back, become a lyric poet again.
Identify with heroes who die for love
and a terrific image,
                    you'll live forever
in your anguished exalted metaphors.
                              Oh yeah.

But remember nature?
                    She takes back all
worn-out lovers,
                    two lie in the earth, one moulders
above-ground;
                    nature is an exhausted mum,
she cant go on forever,
                    this is late
in the machine age.
                    Can you think of one woman
who gave up on the stag line and turned
to God and a peaceful lawn?

Isnt it about time we said to hell with agony?
Shouldnt we be rich with hit parade love by now?
Arent we really free to choose joy over drama,
and havent we come through looking pretty good,
like a line-drive off a perfect swing
in the ninth inning?
                        It leaves the bat faster
than it came to the plate.
                        Taking that pitch
and standing still in the batter's box is nowhere.

Somebody's talking.

                Listen, stupid Kerrisdale heart,
the way your dead heroes listened, till
they were lifted out of their shoes,
but they couldnt hear it all, they thought
they were standing on earth.

                      No,
you're not going to hear the final clap of truth;
that would kill you in two heart-beats.

But listen to the wind in the chestnut trees,
the breath of autumn's bleeding,
                                    the death
of your young heroes.
                        You recall the breeze
across from the station in Florence,
where you saw an amazing name by the door?
Remember the clouds pulled off the face
of Mt. Blanc you saw from the morning window?
Why would the wind reach down to me?

Am I supposed to translate that swishy voice
into some kind of modern law?
Make me their liar even as the chestnuts are?

Deesse dans l'air repandue,
flamme dans notre souterrain!

Yes, I know, it is odd to be away from the world,
dropping all the habits you learned so well;
never bending to look at a rose face to face,
throwing your name away,
free of hands that held you fiercely,
laughing at what you once ached for,
watching all the old connections unravel in space.

Being dead is no bed of roses,
you have so much work piled up in front of you
before the long weekend.
But the folks who are still alive are too quick
to make their little decisions.
The spooks, they tell me, cant tell whether they're moving
among corpses or the fretful living.
The everlasting universe of things rolls
through all minds of all ages in every back yard,
and none of them can hear themselves think.

The ones who left early dont need our voices;
they're weaned from this ground as neatly
as we're diverted from mum's tit. But
what about us?
     We need the mystery, we need
the grief that makes us long for our dead friends,
we need that void for our poems.
We'd be dead without them.

Queen Marilyn made silly movies, but she's
the stuff our words are made from.
                                    Her meaning
struts along the lines of a hundred lovely books.
Her music may be heard in the gaps in the traffic
of 41st Avenue.
                        Her shiny breasts
fill the hands of our weeping poets.

Elegy Two

Dead poets' voices I have heard in my head
are not terrifying.
                    They tell me like lovers
we are worth speaking to,
                    I am a branch
a singing bird will stand on for a moment.

Like a singing branch I call out in return. How
do otherwise?
                    Rather that than couple
with a swan on 41st Avenue.
                            When Hilda
appeared in my dream, she did not visit, she
walked by, into the other room,
                            and I didnt fall
in fear, but in love.

Inside.

Out there was the fortunate fall, mountains
glistening with creation,
                                a glacier between them,
flowing bright out of the working god's fingers,
first orchards rising from the melt, light
shaped on crest and cut,
                                the roll of storms
shaking new trees, flattening the grass,
                                                quick lakes
a scatter of mirrors, clouds in them, all
favour, all breathing side to side, all
being outside,
                all blossom.

As for us, we dissolve into hungers,
                              our breath
disappears every minute,
                              our skin flakes off
and lies unseen on the pavement.
                              She says
I've got you under my skin, yes, she says
you walk with me wherever I go,
                              you are
the weather.

                    I reply with a call for help,
I'm disappearing,
                    there's a change in the weather.

Half the beautiful ones I have known are gone,
what's the hurry?
               On this street the schoolgirls
grow up and disappear into kitchens,
                                    a breeze
shakes the blossoms from my cherry tree,
there's cat hair all over the rug.
                              What happened
to that smile that was on your face
a minute ago?
               God, there goes another breath,
and I go with it,
                    I was further from my grave
two stanzas back, I'm human.
                              Will the universe
notice my unattached molecules drifting thru?

Will the dead poets notice our lines appearing among them,
or are their ears filled with their own music?

Will their faces look as blank as these I pass
on 41ˢᵗ Avenue?
                    I'm not talking about
making that great anthology,
                                        I am recalling that god
who said excuse me, I wasnt listening, sorry.

In love we have a secret language we dont remember.
We catch a word or two,

                     as the wind passes,
we turn an ear to the cool,

                        it's gone. The trees
shake their leaves to say look,

                        we're alive.
The house you've sat in for years remains
against all odds,

               a part of the earth.

We are the wisps,

              we flit invisible
around all that wood.

                  They dont even hear us,
they may be waiting for us to say something important.

Late night on 37th Avenue I see lovers
on each other in a lamplit Chevrolet.

Do their hands know for certain that's skin
they glide over?
                I have rubbed my neck in exhaustion,
and almost believe I've touched something.

Is that a reason to look forward to next year?
Still, being dead
is no bed of roses.

But the moony flesh in the sedan
turns like the firmament,
                              he is entangled
in legs and gearshift,
                              she likely says yes
and grows to meet his growth,
                                        dumb imitation
of the burgeoning garden in the nearby yard.

I grow more frail as they fill the car,
already disappearing,
                              should I ask them
whether I exist?

Si me soubmectz, leur serviteur
En tout ce que puis faire et dire,
A les honnorer de bon cuer

I know they put their hands there and there
because their early fancy now arrives,

                              an island
risen from a placid sea.
                    An actual breast, a leg
that does not disappear below conflicting pictures.

But the ones who have touched me have
disintegrated into seraphs and books.

These half-undressed in the front seat
have nearly slipped from time,
                         elastic hours
making Pleiades of the street.

Yet if they see the morning,

                          safe from their first
rough sea,

            if they smooth each other's hair,
talk about their weekend shopping – are they
what they were?

                 Are they as far from time?

Do they kiss, and try to kiss again, and say
inside, yes I remember this?

                    Does a mask
feel the touch of a mask;

                 does the face
beneath the mask feel the mask?

Did you see ancient Fred and whitened Ginger
in the morning paper,
                    June 25, 1982? Now
each time we see them glide by each other's
garments in black & white youth, we stand
amazed.
            How light that touch, how quick,
how foreign to the dull surge of our own passion,
we thought.
                They generated enormous energy, yet
met like eyelashes.
                They were exactly like us.

God, should he choose,
                    can press us into
sausage patties,
                he can flatten a car,
furl up a street,
                tuck us into our own shoes.

We step out of cars, finally,

                    movies come to an end,
we need a place at last that will fit us,
we need a cabin, a creek, a few trees,
maybe a typewriter and a sink.

                      We are evaporating
as our heroes did.

                We cannot pursue our fragments
as they separate into earth and stars.

Elegy Three

Love is yearning for the stars,
                          love is yearning
by the night stars for a body full of blood.

Send a dozen love poems into the late air
and where are you?
                  The deep shame in the body,
the ancient, rude-formed cave god in the blood
she may suspect but never see;
                          he blushes with hunger
she knows nothing about.

What a vulnerable thing she is
in her crisp white summer dress.

He swims noisily in his black red ocean,
grunting and blowing,
                    a comic book horror of a sea lion.

His snorting echoes off the rocks
ashore.
        The night sky appears and recoils,
                                    the stars
move back an inch.
                    They smile in their own
surrounding dark,
                they know themselves.
                                    In a moment
he is a gentle swain looking like a sky
into her accepting eyes.

Thou art lightning and love, she says,
but the hunger in his face is not for her, nor
was it given at his birth.
                              His thick lips
around your nipple, girl, are not sucking you alone.

You are a wisp,
                    your sudden coming moves him
only to the beginning of his passion,
                                        he is in you,
yes, and now he is thru you.

True, you caught his breath with your fingers,
but that groan you heard,
                              that frightened lunge
ran across the ether and up his spine,
                                        he's gone.

Say his name and only his corpse will reply.
Only his body and the nearest part of his soul
will make a home in your warmth.

He is your child,
                    except for the dark area behind his eyes,
he will grow in your garden,
he will be new for you.

He was new for his Kerrisdale mum,
                              he grew
like a poppy in her garden.
                    She kept him in after dark,
safe from midnight vapours.
                        He was her
riddle of bones.
                    She was his tidy doorway,
keeping him safe,
                      showing him his new world
a little at a time.
                    She gave him a wooden gun
when he was eight.
                      She read him stories
in which children win
                      but grow up anyway.

She held him in the middle of her own slight spasm,
a magnesium flash that swallowed the shadow
behind the door,
                    the shadow that looked around then
just like his adult body today.
                                        Stars
cast faint but ineradicable shadows.

Curtains can be drawn by mum
before she goes to her own bed.

Lying in the dark becoming lighter he scents the perfume
he knows also from your purse,
                              he feels
the approach of his other mother sleep,
                                        this family
is sweeter than anything he will know,
he is safe, you think;
                        but where he is going
someone is typing up the code for the first
season of the world.
                    You see he sleeps, a
passive vacancy present here,
                              he sleeps,
but he dreams too;
                    and where he now soars
there are no mothers,
                      there are only
stellar monsters to be loved,
                              there are galaxies
of fire just missing the cockpit.
                                  He is inside,
where you have been but can never enter.

He loves the terror prior to earth life.
                                        You
would hate it if you knew.
                              He loves
the collapsing bridge he is running upon.

In his dream inside his dream he knows he will
make it,
              step to the edge of green ground
the moment the crash will sound.
                                    You smile
at his rolling eyelids as you back out of his room.

He's back again among the gruesome beings
who welcome him,
                        who smile with bleeding lips,
whose eyes search him out,
                        whose ancient brittle eyes
he smiles into.
                Before you turn
you see a smile fleet on his face.
                                Your heart
warms as you walk downstairs to your vegetables.

You love his dream you do not know.
                                He
is among the dreadful ancestors he knew
before you felt him kick inside your womb.

The young woman steps from the car,
                                        her feet
among flowers.
                    She thinks she is a new love.

But we do not love anything new.
                                    You lift
in me a cool green earth,
                            home of all my dead loves,
a blonde Pictish girl of unexplainable beauty,
glimpsed on her daily walk in my farthest sleep,
a sea of dead sailors,
                        the valley of their mothers,
my heart filled with living voices
heard by the ears of Cygnus.
                            Last winter
on the train thru Carrara I heard them
for a second,
                and the train is running today.

As I watch you walk,
                        your white dress
falling around your thighs in the starlight,
I love you for everybody you have been.

I dont care whether your mother is waiting up for you.

Mother, you have lovers too,
                    they stir in their armour.

The flush you feel comes from ancient eyes on your back.

Men are beating each other below Mount Cyllene
for the right to bring you an asphodel.

Widows detest you,
                    their grown children lust for you.

A gentle painter caught you
in that quattrocento oil you saw in Florence last December.

When he comes downstairs in the morning,
                                    his eyes
asquint against the window light,
                              bring his berries
from the yard,
                  hug him for the warmth from his bed,
promise him an afternoon at the beach.

The stars will be out of the sky
                              till long past supper time.

Elegy Four

These high chestnut branches along Larch Street
fade above the streetlights,
                                  live without me.

A truck passes in the morning,
                                  it is full summer,
and a flock of noisy starlings leaps into the sky.

I jump from my top step,
                                  and sprawl on the lawn,
eyeglasses bouncing twice along the walk.

I dont know what time of year it is,
                                  I flower
and die each afternoon.
                              A muscular dog trots by,
certain where he's going.

I follow one scent,
                    sure of my appetite,
but am distracted by a crossing spoor.
                              My nature
is torn,
        I am a trespasser,
                  I promised to
steer clear,
        stay in my own territory,
                        but love
makes intruders,
        I am not I here,
                  but the burglar
of your past.

'I' dont even see you till the light blinks
and a white backdrop appears behind you.

It hurts the eye that turns to rest on you.

Inside I am a blind mystery,
                          only my skin
knows what is happening.

I've stood before the oven door my heart
is baking in, wondering,

                how will it come out?

Will it burn before the buzzer goes,
will silly images fill my anxiety waiting here?

When I take it out will it make the guests
go ahh,

           another Kerrisdale satisfaction?

The trees outside the kitchen window
know the shape of the wind in their roots,
and I'm standing here,

              sniffing for smoke.

What am I doing in the kitchen?

I'd rather be upstairs with my toys.
                              I know
how they work.
                    I dont mind their fake colours.

I'll spend hours with my toy trucks,
play in the dark,
                        listen to the hiss of the trees.

I dont care whether my spooky ancestors
sit on the floor with me,
                              gruesome beings.

They can remain the other side of the collapsing bridge
between those stars,
                            they can call me over,
I dont care.
              Here I stay.

                          I can listen to them
like a radio in the dark.

At my father's funeral I held my mother's hand
and my sister's fierce hand,
                              and heard my father's voice.

It's all right, the words in my quiet head,
it's all right,
              and I half believed him,
                                        half believed
them.

        I was born dead centre of the depression,
grew up watching him settle for less,
                                    watching him
read less as time wore on and there was more real furniture.

I spent hours with him devoid of speech,
carrying wood, throwing a ball, flipping a card,
hours growing an attachment that would not speak.

I speak to him now in all my poems,
                                    my body
speaks to him every time I look at it.
                            He is silent,
aware of my ambition but as in my childhood
tolerant of my forms.
                    Asking only that I know work,
that I come to his station;
                        so I remember his calling
each time I toil unbidden in the yard.

It's all right.

Upstairs with my toys – a pen, some lined paper,
my books open around me.

                            I am staring at this sound
coming out blue, so hard,
                      another voice
must mix with its own,
                a dead poet or father.

So there are three of us,
                    who divide the world
by remaining apart,
                come together on these
rare occasions,
             funeral of the trees
                          (one voice said this,
the others assented in the saying).

The gruesome gone hear us in moments like this,
the wheel descending to their chambers.

                                            They laugh
derisively,
                they know how seldom we come together.

They know that we will walk apart
for most of the year.
                        We court them thus
and they say 'nice try,'
                      though by then we are gone again,
back to the kitchen,
                  back to the grave,
back into a book more often mentioned than open.

My childhood's toys never grew cool from my gone touch.
They were presents,
                              they had no history but mine.
They fell into shapes on the floor,
                                        constellations
observed in Cathay and Tical.
                              Voices murmured around them.

They would disappear when I learned
to buy my own books.
I was in no hurry to grow,

                    or so I thought,
                                        but I moved to where the stars
were fewer,
              I carried my books and magazines with me.

I was always the youngest and the best read.
I wanted not to please my elders but to annoy them,
by exceeding their speed,
                          by leaping
past their adulthood,
                        child's skin on my face.

Most of all I loved my solitude,
                                hoping another
somewhere did the same,
                                and another somewhere
between toys and the world soon to be made.

I knew my solitude was pictured between stars,
knew a long-dead vizier read it on a screen
and approved,
                        as no parent could.

Déjà l'odeur bouge en des orages gonflés
Suinte sous le pas des portes
Aux chambres secretes et rondes,
Là où sont drésses les lits clos.

Can I show you that sole child behind his own door?
Point to where he rides between two stars
considering his path?

                         Is it I who has to
whiten his hair,
                    narrow his arteries, perhaps
put a bullet between his shoulders?
                                    That could be
easy, lock me up,
                    forget what cell I'm in.

But each step he takes before he thinks of walking
is a step toward the grave,
                         a step down
into the earth.

                    He carries his shroud with him
on the first day of school.

                    Think of that
and ask for a book of musical thought!

Elegy Five

For a few hours,
             for a summer,
                          we think we know them,
these young men in three-coloured caps,
                          playing
the game of boyhood,
             brief in our eyes.

Do they play for us,
             or are they performing
the ancient demands of their decorated bodies?

They wear their names on their backs,
but they wear costumes designed a century past,
of gentlemen meeting of a Sunday on the grass.

The white ball acts upon them as a stone in a pool.
They run, they bend, they leap, they fall
to the patchy green carpet,
walled away from the factory city.

The eye up high for a moment catches
a soft human Diamond,

                              a star
twinkt in a moment by the hurl, the ex-
stacy of the thing among them.

                              The giant at first
leaps then tumbles,
                    his feet quick to return
to artificial earth.

                    What holds him there
is not anywhere.

The crowd opens,
                rises like a row of poppies,
and subsides,
                scattering peanut shells like petals.

They surround the never-dying game,
a stem that feeds their seeming boredom,
the late innings,
                the mum at home
basting a roast.
                Children stray thru the stands,
faces away from the centre.

A thin fine play in the eighth
draws a flutter of hands.

The wrinkled neck of the third base coach
mocks his uniform,
                    or vice versa.
He wears no spikes,
                    but shoes like slippers.
His stomach falls over his double-knit belt.

His statistics lie like the skeleton of another man
in yearbooks out of print.

He never stands in the coach's box, as if
afraid it might be a grave.

Beauty is the first prod of fear,
                              the young
shortstop knows it but does not say it.
                                   Tobacco
bulges his cheek,
                  his movement speaks
of his parentage,
                  a swan and a gangster.

He is simple for three hours.

He knows the ground between his feet.

You play thru your injuries,
                           you play
hurt,
        you knew it was waiting for you,
you remember your first bad arm,
it said your pension would be full of pain.

You hit the ground every day,
knocked over in the middle of your grace,
a green apple hitting every branch
on the way to the sun-beaten orchard floor;

your team-mates' play called it into being,
                                   your fall
seen a hundred times on the screen,
a way down, and out.
                    You bounce up
without a smile,
                but the crowd says 'ahh,'
and you look quick at your manager,
                                dad,
were you watching me.

                    He is looking in his book,
but your sore body grins
all the way back to the dugout,
unaware of your steps over the grave.

Already the stands are noisy
with the call for some hitting,
                            the home half
cuts the pain from your knees,
                            your heart
hides in the shade,
                hoping the pitcher
will serve unwritten fate,
                        your wooden friend
will find a fatness,
                you will run
to throw yourself to earth again,
                            let me in.

Baseball angel,
   it's early summer,
      accept him,
lighten the air,
   open the infield,
     give him
one white rainbow today,
    set him on second,
the lovely red dirt all over his flannel.

Extra
basis.

And shine bright shadows on the tan skin
of that sweetheart with the odd designation:
ball girl.

   I watch her blossom these years,
call her Debbie though I dont know her;

she sits in a simple folding chair next to the stands,
glove on her hand,
     blonde hair spilling from her cap,
long tan thighs,
   tall white sox.

She is not baseball at all,
but a harmless grace here,
    a tiny joy
glimpsed one time each inning,
     when she bends
and, oh God give us extra innings,
picks up the ball.

   We applaud, and nature
is good.

Les humains savent tant de jeux l'amour la mourre
L'amour jeu des nombrils ou jeu de la grande oie
La mourre jeu de nombre illusoire des doigts
Seigneur faites Deigneur qu'on jour je m'enamoure

Watching the game of work,
                                    I wonder at the big owe
how dark in my heart is the place where we all
could not make the play,
                            fell to earth crooked,
swung a bat too late,
                                  threw far over the fielder's head,
cringed in fear of the hardness,
or the coach who scorned our fear.

Here is the fancied green of our wishes,
here where I still think the ballplayers are older than I,
this is where they are unreasonably adept,
where our failure is turned inside out,
by quick hands and an always white ball.

I sit in section nine and sometimes wonder why,
but know I am at ground zero
where art is made,
                     where there is no profit,
no loss.

        The planet lies perfect in its orbit.

Diamonds,

        this green diamond at Little Mountain,
where these younger than we leap and run and fall
like our older brothers,

               where we shout inanities
from our high wall,

          our wit echoes loudly
from the right-field fence.

               This is not
poetry,

      neither is it play;

           it is life
whether you like it or not,

            money
changes hands,

        the sun goes purple and gold
behind the trees,

        the lights come on bright,
the ball is white,

        and someone
has to pay for it.

Dear spooks:
                    if there were a domed stadium between the stars
upon whose astroturf athletic lovers
made plays beyond the hearts of these heroes,
daring ozone catches in deepest centre,
                                        stolen base
in a cloud of crystal,
                        delightful silent hand-shakes
at home plate –

                    and if they could arouse the crowd
of long-ghosted millions to a standing ovation,
a thunder-clap around the park,

                                would that throng
cast blossoms of immortality over nine heads,
bring at last a satisfied smile to the face
between these shoulders here on earth,
                                on the road,
in last place?

Elegy Six

Yes, I see you, backyard raspberries,
you've been there
                all my life,
all thru my verse.
                 One day you
spit white blossoms,
                    and when I dont immortalize them
you hang a million heavy cones,
                      your branches droop
to the earth with dark berries;
                 I cant pursue
your quickness.
            The first moment out of sleep, and you
are ecstatic.
           I sit in my pyjamas and read the
kitchen newspaper,
              glance at your pride.
                     A god
could have scampered across the lawn while I was
turned to the stove, looking for coffee.

We hang on,
plugging for fame,
scotch-taping our blossoms to
our already browning stems.
When we produce
at last our final over-ripe fruit,
the earth around us
is already frozen,
the family snug abed for winter.

But we know a few who sprout flames in the dark before morning,
lighting the air we've only learned to breathe,
their godlike voices singing from their still skinny bodies.

We make heroes of them,
      jealously, we know
they are touched,
      they spring the most glorious
green reeds along our rusty lanes,
        they took
the beautiful back road to death.

       They turn
bright circles of colour,
      like the painted bicycle
wheels of Greg Curnoe,
      king child.

ou bien le corps
quand il se prend
pour seul témoin
d'un avenir
impérissable?

You cant catch their breath with your fingers,

                                             heroes

are strange,

                    they are ghosts of the dying young,

they dont care for survival,

                             they rise and spread

being.

           Every flower is an exploding star.

                                      Few

have the nerve to sniff that scent,

                          I never

drove out of Kerrisdale into Death Valley in my

dead hero's time bomb automobile.

                                I never heard

the detonation behind his blue eyes.

In twenty years I've never heard his like.

                                       But last night
the first fall wind cut the bamboo beside my window,
and his black song entered,

                           rattling the papers off my desk.

Beauty is the first prod of fear –
                              I would escape
this awful longing.
                    I want to be a kid
with all this before me,
                         Georgie on the rug, reading
of Jesus,
         eyeing my mother,
                            wondering whether she knows.

Mary mother of Pearl,
                 he was a hero in your womb.

He began the swift race there,
                   he chose you for his
irritating arena.
             Envy pulsed in a thousand other bellies,
as he chose a stance,
             flexed and began.
                       His first miracle
was his escape from your dark embrace
                  into this awful longing.

You mothers of the bright flash,

                     before you can imagine,

the upstairs bedroom is empty at night,

                          your house

is for a moment ringed in a glow of blossoms,

                              stars

rain on the roof,

             suicides attest to the fearsome

beauty of your issue.

             You had a quick joy.

There were no witnesses,
            then a million.

                        Each word of love
moved your son a mile,
            each loving hand touched him
like the wind.

            When they saw him raise his arms at the tape
he was no racer but erased;

in his place the blinking corner of a constellation.

Elegy Seven

No more love poems for you,
                              dear old voice,
you've outgrown them here on this street of leaves.

I know,
        I know, you can still do it,
                              turn words
as those swallows turn quick in the air they know.

But each of them falls and is eaten,
                              and you
are only consumed.

                    Even while pretty ears listen
you rise above them,
                    past those handy trees, looking
for a listener who has not announced herself.

You speak a language you are only now learning,
hoping she will hear you,
                          knowing she is yourself
out there.

Lightning and love,
                              if spring were here
she would listen and nod her head,
                              your music
would announce her erotic shape everywhere.

                                        First

her naked ankle,
                    your first words,
                                        and then still
weak silver sun gathered round her filmy dress,
your stanzas made an everywhere.

                              She walks

and rises,
              flowers in the sky round her hair,
blossoms her cape,
              blooms where she has stepped,
your music made colour.

You swell your lungs
and invent summer,
                    up at earlier light, up
before the heavy trees,
                    spilling heat down those mountains
to ripple over the pavement of 41st Avenue,
                                        bring
shop women to the sidewalk for air.
                            Others are
zipping by on bikes,
                    powerful thighs brown in the sun,
power everywhere,
                    boys crashing into third base
at Elm Park,
                old geezers with gentleman shoulders
rolling heavy orbs over pressed turf,
                                late afternoon
meeting of hips,
                bedsheets thrown into a corner.

Powerful voice,
               the summer nights here, in summer
the night belongs to earth at last,
                    those stars
are thrown into space from earth.

                  We should
go among them,
           learn them all,
                    know especially
the roads between them.

               We should never forget them.

They are made from dead poets' voices.

I've called,

        I've sung to a lover,

                        but when she appeared
she brought with her a team of womanly figures,
shapes risen from remembered graves.

                    One's voice
belongs to them all,

        they all want to rise to earth again.

Dear children to come,

        remember these words above all else:
what you live all your life to be,

        you are now.

You will scamper after your love,

        win the race,
and run smiling,

        your chest heaving,

           where you are now,
before freedom,

        in the open.

Where you are now.
                         It is lovely to be here.
Even you know that,
                         you women lost in your familiar
dirty coats in front of a broken door,
                              a pissy hotel
on East Hastings,
                   rain on passing cop cars, somewhere
you know it.
               For each of you there was an hour,
there was a long minute,
                    a time I can measure
with half a line,
                when your eyes were wide enough
for your soul to leap out,
                stand and say

yes,
   here I am,
        I am.
            Entire.
                You felt it beating
against your nerve-ends.

                But you and I do forget
what the people across the lawn can never see,
what they may never desire of us.
                  No, we have to
turn it outside,
              we want everyone to see it, we
forget the lovely world we have been dying to see
is still inside;
             we have to transform it
in the open,
        inside.

Dans l'onde toi devenue
Ta jubilation nue.

Corny, isnt it?
           The world turns within us,
while we transform it,
              fancy words but true,
sweetheart.

        The alleged world outside fades before our eyes.

Remember that big house at 38th and Larch?
Look now:
        a translucent spectre rises there,
                   comfortable
as the notion of home still building in your brain.

So all your neighbours have built this city block,
ethereal as their own passing conversations.

                       They
would put leaves on their naked pear trees.

They build a stadium of the heart downtown,
and will never find their way to the game.

But you and I,
        as they say,
                you and I will keep our hearts'
architecture in secret;

             if one structure deserved praise,
if once it was turned to with humble love,
we preserve it where it will never be razed, in-
visible.

        Nearly everyone walks by it as the eye
past a dark star,
          poor sad bozos, their hearts
empty,
        finding no familiar temple to bow down to
and imagine,
         inside where the outside is.

Poor sad *insensatti*,
                 I see them in Kerrisdale and Trieste;

each time our heavy earth turns its outside to the dark sky,
it carries idiots who have given up the past
and lost the future.

               Poor men,
                     even tomorrow is beyond sight.

But you and I dont have to discard our eyes, our
open eyes preserve the form we still recognize.

This, This, This
               stood in the city's heart,
                      stood
in the storm of chance,
               it stood there
while the streets evaporated,
                 it stood where
light from a million stars converged.

I'll show it to you,
                 it's there now,
                                  we took it down
brick by brick and rebuilt it here,
                                  we build it every day,
I'll take you there,
                 it's here where you
have eyes to see.

          Look up,
                      if you can imagine, up
there,
          the light on the roof above that darkened town.

How's that for 'glistening with creation'?

                                        Isnt that
a wonder?
              Human expression, human desire.

                                        Go back to the stars
and tell them about that,
                      tell them in your language,
I'm out of breath,
                 I couldnt begin …

Tell them
we're not dead yet,
                    not while we honour the space inside,
rebuild the luminous palace there.

                        Palace?
                                The gymnasium
of our veins.

            It must be enormous.
                                After five thousand years
There is running room on the floor.

That shining roof,
                    you must see it from your abode,
you must be able to look thru the top windows.

Our songs must reach your highway between the stars.

But that young woman,
                            staggering with love
from the parked car to her door –
                                I think her hair
has to brush across your leg.

But no more love songs for you,
I said,
        you wouldnt listen anyway,
                        would you?

My song says I'm holding you
off,
        remember?

                That hand I hold toward you
is not open,
                it is a fist under your nose,
I'm not one with you yet.

                        I'll stay here awhile,
go to lunch in Kerrisdale,
                        wonder what edifice
can glow within the hurried waitress.

Elegy Eight

FOR MICHAEL ONDAATJE

Today I saw two robins feeding on worms along Yew Street,
eyes wide,
           looking into the open air, they
were not beset by past and future and wishfulness.

All animals see with their eyes what is before them.

But we look elsewhere,
                  our eyes bind things
to our desires,
            our fears mock the great trees
in this neighbourhood.

               Oh oh, says the anxious reviewer,
this poet is not in control of his materials.

Only by watching the birds fly do we know
there is sky between the trees.

        I force my daughter
to learn the names of the continents, names
that snare the past.
     That's how we stay living
over centuries.

     The robin sees me coming,
          his act
is not fear,
    he moves only to keep his eye on me.

He will eat and fly and die,
       and reach eternity
without naming it.

We dissolve into hungers,
our breath disappears every minute,
                              we can measure
our remaining store with a hand-held calculator.

Not for a day do we live only in space,
where windflowers open without history.
                              We live on a wheel,
never in Sunyatta, where the lungs rest
un-numbered.

                    I see my daughter's body come to rest,
her eyes set somewhere I envy,
                              and like a miserly Latin master,
I wave my fingers before her face.
                              I'm afraid
she's visiting the domain of not-being,
not-bothering-to-be,
                    damn it, what a coward.
To sneer at the meditating cat,
                              to avoid the face
of the nearly dead,
                    who looks like an animal in peace.

We remember getting there while making love,
                                        nearly,
to losing all care,
            to the open,
                        where all that matters
falls away, nearly.
                Where only the other body
keeps us here.

                We come back finally
to looking at the watch on the familiar wrist,
reaching for the cigarette,
                    horizontal clichés,
                            remembering
where the underwear is,
                moving an awkward elbow
that keeps us from being nowhere.

                          The open had been
just beyond her,
            but you were in her, she
is after all,
            the world.

As I walk past the hedges of Kerrisdale all I see
is a translation of the open,

                       nature to our advantage
pressed,
         or the natural eye of a robin
looking past me to the sky.

                Stupid fate,
to be nothing more than this,
                 a foreign timetable,
an unwanted designer trampling the woods.

Des forces que tu tiens ta liberté dispose,
Mais de tous tes conseils l'univers est absent.

If this hairy dog trotting down Yew Street
knew what I know,

     he'd get my ass in his teeth
and never let go.

    But he knows what his nose does,
and sees the first few feet of eternity.

        I know
the fiction of my past and expect to walk
straight into my fancied future.

      He walks,
we see indulgently,

    on an angle,

      from bush to bush;
when we see a busy dog walk straight and quick,
we say how like a man.

Dog and robin,

   we made no streets for you.

Yet look again at the dog's hanging head,
                                    a weight
we think we know lies on his neck.

                        All memories
are sad,
        he has them too,
                    is this true?

                            We look
with whipped expectation for something
we used to curl up in,
                    turn in circles three times
and lie down.

            It was tender.
                        We slept. Without
open eye we nuzzled and there we were.

                            Here
we have to run to reach,
                    but do we reach?

There – remember? – it was enough to breathe.
                                    Home
was next to a loud heart.
                    Now we are in the street
too long for our feet.

Ah, those lucky little beings who never leave mother,
burrow in a womb that is world.
                              These curled
insects that live under the tatters of my gladiola,
fetal,
        knowing all they touch was there
when they were born.

                    That happy robin again,
seems to know,
                    he may bounce or fly,
                                    in a matrix
that includes the sky.

                    He does not know he is
the image of a pedestrian heart,
                              come from
a belly near another heart,
                              here to chatter between trees,
tipping wing,
        skidding across his own wakened air,
like a pen across a modern poem.

Let us go then,
          heart and eye,
                   to look as always,
attend as always,
            look at the world and never
out of it.

        It begins to fall down a little.
We renovate and proudly show our friends.

Cracks appear, and we patch them.
                        Cracks appear in us
and our friends appear to watch.
                  To be
watching.

        Dogs walk by;
              birds fly, away.

Why do I keep getting lost this way,
                                four blocks
from home,
                or is it a city away?
                                I get turned around,
no matter what street I take,
                                so I always look
like a man saying goodbye.

                                Like a banished citizen
allowed one last look at Kerrisdale,
                                yellow leaves
falling on lawns,
                I hesitate,
                                trying to remember it all,
every day the same farewell.

Goodbye, warm world
who gave me birth
and told me
not to stick around.

Elegy Nine

The laurel bush grows enormous, nearly obliterating
the front steps and pouring its dark waxy leaves over
into the porch.

        I never sit there, though I could,
there are two Yankee Stadium seats on the porch.

I could sit there,
        reading poetry,
            imitating
that robust companion,
        reading, perhaps, Mallarmé.

            But they said I had to be
human,
    running from doom,
        longing for fortune.

Half the beautiful ones I have known are gone.

My longing is not for happiness –
                                        that only proves

your days are leaving one by one.

                            Not even to see
what's in the mail this morning.

                        Not just
to get the sap running,
                            any bush can do that.

Because here this once I can be bound to
meaning,
            because it looks as if the world wanted me,
the disappearing neighbourhood needs my step.

I will be the first to go,
                    my one chance spent so quick.

One for you, too.
                One chance to offer to the world
meaning.

            No second stanza to develop,
                            you'd better
write a good first verse.

                    But you could have
died in the womb,
                you did get this one blank page.

No eraser can undo your visit.

On my dresser upstairs you'll find a limestone pebble
I brought across the sky from a cliffside path
at Duino.

       I'll leave it here when I go,
                                   along with
everything else.

       Just so,
                 we run over the earth,
carry pieces of it in our hands,
                      so we squeeze it
and demand meaning,
                 we urge it to resemble our heart.

I brought eleven pieces of Duino home with me
and gave away ten,
                 but think the one I retain
is really me,
          I havent given away anything.

I want to keep it in my bedroom forever.

Importun
Vent qui rage!
Les défunts?
Ça voyage.

Our words will stay – maybe – pebbles to tell of our pain,
the hard path we had to walk for a few years,
the long long moments of love,
                                                        or trying to love.

Things that could never be told,
                                                 so we gave words instead.

Stranger yet the nights we got out from under the street lamps,
could see the still,
                                    stars at least,
                                                        feel
a little homesick.

                                    Then we knew enough to come back empty.

No one brings a stone away from that home.

I came back in the morning,
                                   eyes half open,
                                                to say
chestnut tree, laurel bush, cherry, front porch, eyes
open,
         to tell bird, window, lover, determined insect
happily burrowed in the earth round these gladioli.

To count them and bind them to life,
                                     to praise
them and energize the earth.

                                   Those lovers in the car
are seduced not by each other but by secret earth
filled with proper desire for transfiguration.

                                   That I
should say such a word in a poem.

                                   They kiss
and feel the press of more than their own flesh,
they are happy to add their hot hands
to the never-ending shaping and praising of the world.

The trick of the dance is in following,
now the words,
allegro,
         now the contrary beat of the glossy leaf.

It is time to speak now,
                              to say the words that are
ready,
          to name the world we can still see,
                                        the leaves
depart their tree but the tree is here.

                                   Speak, praise,
before the tree is gone with your going,
                                        before
you become act without words.

                         It is no bed of roses,
being dead.
             Your silent blood is a message
from a dying messenger.
                         It is filled with words
your tongue can move into sound,
                         words your neighbourhood deserves.

The ghastly dead will never applaud your imitation of them,
your beautiful silence.

They wrote the book on silence.

They own the rights to invisible meaning.

                                              Show them
something made of earth,
                              bring out the foot stool
your father made in high school shop,
                                        a necklace
your grandmother bought from a Haida fisherman;

things,
          made by hands and real as their names.

Say look at these marvels,
                            we did these, we
have eyes and hands,
                        our best poet said
the optic heart must venture.

                              They will stare
and applaud,
              as you did,
                          watching
the father and son on Querétaro Street bending cane
to make chairs till the light fell up the walls.

Praise our things.

           They are innocent in our hands,
the sweet pain of Archie Shepp's tenor saxophone
lives for fingers and ears,
                show them how we love,
how we grace the earth a horn is fashioned from.

The earth,
        how it requires us to live,
                  how it
desires to become us.

           How the ash trees along Larch Street
turn to me for their life,
             to this ephemeron in running shoes.

All right,
            I hear you,
                        I know you want to grow again
in another soil,
            if that's what I am.
                                    To disappear
and live again in me.
                        All your seasons have been
practice transformations.
                        Is this possible?
                                    Am I
going mad in Kerrisdale?
                        Lightning and love,
if spring comes again she will nod her head
in my heart –
            all right, I agree,
                                    you may die
and move in.
            I will give you a new name.

Another mouth to feed,
                        what's that?
                                    I was a child,
God knows what I'll be tomorrow.
                                    Now I'm a new
husband,
            now I am something like two.

Elegy Ten

Est-ce toi, Nomade, qui nous passeras ce soir aux
rives du réel?

If I endure, when this ghastly truth has passed my eyes,
may I raise music to my dead family in the dark.

Lift this light horn and play a song I know but
have never learned,
                              fingers touching keys I cannot see
through tears I always knew were there.

                                        Remember
when we were kids,
                              how we wept and secretly
loved our tears?

              How wise we were,
                                        children see
where they are going.
                              How their parents and teachers
mock them,
              drilling, memorizing happy little songs.

In November the wind slides in from the sea
and eats at our faces.

                              We should smile and bow,
it is the air of a sweet and terrible quartet.
                                                      Precious

agony.

              How we threw away half our lives
waiting like cows for better weather.

                                                      Suffering
is our winter of bare branches,
                                        our secret abode.

So we walk like strangers in Kerrisdale streets,
feet sore in our shoes,
                          forehead aching from our
squint in the rain.

                    The slapping of car tires on wet street
resounds from walls and fences,
                              engines droning
on the next block,
                    noise folding into noise till
we hear nothing but the occasional climbing DC-10.

We are inside an enormous overturned empty cup.

The shingled Anglican church across 37th Avenue,
highrises filled with perfumed widows asleep,
cosy women's-wear shoppes on 41st,
                                    all
could be flattened by one ghost stepping off
the road between the stars.

But all winter the parks will be green,
                              and in the parks
the shades of kids and dads,
                              running from base to base,
throwing balls,
                    falling over dogs,
                                    dutifully dropping
ice cream wrappers in trash barrels,
                                    a lot of
shouting under trees filled with the shades of leaves.

(And across the field,
                    real estate plotters wondering
who to bribe,
                    to grab all that green and call it
undeveloped.)

Later in the bars on Hastings Street
dads and others down that lovely gold stuff,

                                                get gold

into their veins,
                    find something to laugh about,

                                          avoid

falling chairs,
          and convince themselves they'll never die.

They'll get into a car in two o'clock rain but never die.
There's a traffic cop called Real Death but he's
on the other side of town,
                    where strangers are assholes.

In the after-hours joint full of smoke children are playing guitars,
lovers are propped against their alien clothes,
the toilet flushes endlessly behind the thin wall.

A slightly drunk dad is amazed by the different beauty
of a thin young woman with sorrow in her eyes.

It takes a while to determine that she's here alone,
she doesnt have a car,
                              her thin shoulders implore, they
demand to be nuzzled.
                        She's too good for this place.

With a stupid remark he begins a conversation
whose intention is to find out whether he can afford
to take her home.

                    Even when she says she lives
on the road between the stars,
                              he finds cause
to think she's lovely.
                        But he also thinks that he
is stupid.

                    He buys another tequila screwdriver
and drifts,
                    and drives home to early morning Kerrisdale,
his windshield wipers crossing the wet snow in her eyes.

Like an old singing branch I call out,
                                            but only
those who died in their first cantos follow her home.

Dying girls and dying boys,
                                            they follow her home.

Girls envy her rich diaphanous comet tail dress,
boys hold her sweet cold hand,
                                            walking from her car.

They are at last near the abode where the immortals are
all as beautiful as she,
                        the ghastly company,
                                            refusing
a closing couplet.

All as beautiful,
    and all with sorrowful eyes;

             one
more proximate than the rest converses with the young
visitor,
   the newly dead.

      We were all strong like you,
she says,
   all like you fit to be praised.

We made this place by our coming here,
         we worked
with what was left.
     We drew from our own eyes
the molecules laid on one another for this city.

She signalled to some others who joined them
as they walked about the streets.

                     Look, she said,
at the tall apartments held aloft by faint sighs
drifting from the mouths of lorn pensioners in their rooms.

She gestured to the tall trees,
                         their brilliant limbs
fashioned from tears,
                    the bordering flowers grown only
out of pain.

              Every back yard is prowled by cats
with eyes of sharp grief,
                   fixed on birds
that fill the trees and rooftops with songs of their agony.

Only in a shaded chamber of his stilled mind
does this youth realize he has been strolling through
Kerrisdale
   and around the earth.

He does not recognize me as he passes with his escort,
nor do I see him.

     Only the breeze fails in saying
what it half wants me to hear,
        on the shores of the real.

When light slips up the walls and away,

                                        they lead him

to the graveyard on 41st Avenue,

                              eerie tautology

in a neighbourhood of unseen grannies,

                                    glistening

with decreation.

                   And as all the light races skyward

to settle as tight calligraphy on the black dome above,

they walk with him to the school ground on the hill

and bid him read.

                    He sees,

                        it is an unfolded road map,

ghastly brother to the grid he's made of his life in secret,

a call to greater travel,

                        a total denial of abode.

When he lifts his eyes to look there,

                              he knows

he is truly gone.

A new ghost,
            his half-wrinkled brain out of sync,
he cannot see the neighbourhood clear.

                        But she
tells the narrative of the newly dead to its hero –

a black bird in the dark night descends like the last leaf
from the chestnut tree outside his unseen house,
past his open unseeing eyes,
                        past his alert ear,
offering a song where no bird sings at night on earth,
a short poem of unwelcome comfort,
                        a direction
to read where reading erases the words
line by line,
            street by street.

Till the last page opens onto the earth
beyond his darkened acres,
                           above invisible branches.

Every star becomes a coal as he reads it,
                                        figures
turning to ashes:
                    the Archer, the Scribe,
the one he's always called the Infielder, to the south
the Triestino,
                    quickly followed by the Coyote,
the Wine Glass, Erato, the three-armed Saguaro.

Last to go,
              drawing his reluctant gaze,
the clear white diamonds of the Number Nine.

Love is yearning for the stars,
                              they will
come on again inside the committed dead.

                                        Time falls from him
as he follows his vaporous guides as far as they may go.

You have walked along this street,
                              their beautiful leader tells him,
most of your life,
                    you recognize that dark doorway,
and that.

          In the morning the shopkeepers
will not see you
                  but feel your presence in the wind,
make satisfied jests about the season's immediate cold.

She looks at him a last time with her lorn eyes
and he is alone.

He walks out of Kerrisdale a last time,

                                    not turning to look

but seeing it all.

               The sun rises unknown to him.

His feet no longer feel the pavement.

                         If he did cry out,

none would hear.

But as he goes,
              his going lifts our eyes;
                         we see
a little more from time to time.

                  November sun
on the maple's cushioning moss,
              bamboo canes
across the corner of a window,
                  he leaves us this;

we rush to call it meaning.

We see every thing's entry,
                     the robins that sing,
                              la la,
the muscular dog that trots down our street the first time,

each quick appearance is a farewell.

The single events that raise our eyes and stop our time
are saying goodbye, lover,
                     goodbye.

Kerrisdale Elegies was previously published by Coach House Press in 1984 and in a limited, numbered edition of 82 copies by pooka press in January 2008.